365 Days of Happiness: Inspirational Quotes To Live by

Foreword by
M.G. Keefe

365 Days of Happiness:

Inspirational Quotes for Everyone

Hot Tropica Books Publication

April 2013

Copyright © 2013 Foreword by M.G. Keefe

Cover illustration copyright © Jackson Falls

ISBN 13: 978-1484005187

ISBN: 148400518X

All characters in this book have no existence outside the imagination of the author and have no relation whatsoever to anyone bearing the same name or names. They are not even distantly inspired by any individual known or unknown to the author, and all incidents are pure invention.

Published by: **Hot Tropica Books**

365 Days of Happiness

Blurb:

Finding true joy in life shouldn't be a treasure hunt. Enjoy this collection of quotes, based on appreciating life's pleasures and finding happiness. 365 quotes to make you laugh, smile and cry.

"The Constitution only guarantees the American people the right to pursue happiness. You have to catch it yourself." ~ Author unknown

Foreword by MG Keefe

Happiness can't be bought, or paid for, or wrapped up with a bow and given as a gift. Happiness is something we all must discover on our own.

Some people may believe that happiness will come to us when we get what we want out of life. If we marry, we will become happy. If we have children, it will satisfy that emptiness within. If we only...yes, that list of if only's goes on and one endless.

But none of this is really true, for if the person doesn't already know how to be happy another person won't be able to make up for this. We have to learn how to be content with our lives and appreciate what we have already. There are many ways we can do this.

Yet it will always come down to the simplest of things. We must learn to find true joy in life's gifts.

Happiness must come from within.

365 Days of Happiness

Day 1: Happiness is not something ready made. It comes from your own actions. ~ Dalai Lama

Day 2: If you want to be happy, be. ~ Leo Tolstoy

Day 3: Most people would rather be certain they're miserable, than risk being happy. ~ Robert Anthony

Day 4: Happiness is excitement that has found a settling down place. But there is always a little corner that keeps flapping around. ~ E.L. Konsiburg

Day 5: Happiness is always a by-product. It is probably a matter of temperament, and for anything I know it may be glandular. But it is not something that can be demanded from life, and if you are not happy you had better stop worrying about it and see what treasures you can pluck from your own brand of unhappiness. ~ Roberstons Davies

Day 6: What a wonderful life I've had! I only wished I realized it sooner. ~ Colette

Day 7: Those who can laugh without cause have either found the true meaning of happiness or gone stark raving mad. ~ Norm Paernick

Day 8: Man is fond of counting his troubles, but he does not count his joys. If he counted them up as he ought to, he would see that every lot has enough happiness provided for it. ~ Fyodor Dostoevsky

Day 9: Happiness is never stopping to think if you are. ~ Palmer Sondreal

Day 10: Be kind whenever possible. It is always possible. ~ Dalai Lama

Day 11: If only we'd stop trying to be happy we could have a pretty good time. ~ Edith Wharton

Day 12: People are often unreasonable and self-centered. Forgive them anyway. If you are kind, people may accuse you of ulterior motives. Be kind anyway. If you are honest, people may cheat you. Be honest anyway. If you find happiness, people may be jealous. Be happy anyway. The good you do today may be forgotten tomorrow. Do good anyway. Give the world the best you have and it may never be enough. Give your best anyway. For you see, in the end, it is between you and God. It was never between you and them anyway. ~ Mother Teresa

Day 13: For every minute you are angry, you lose sixty seconds of happiness. ~ Ralph Waldo Emerson

Day 14: Happiness is the meaning and purpose of life, the whole aim and end of human existence. ~ Aristotle

Day 15: I felt my lungs inflate with the onrush of scenery— air, mountains, trees, people. I thought, "This is what it is to be happy." ~ Sylvia Plath

Day 16: I must learn to be content with being happier than I deserve. ~ Jane Austen

Day 17: I'd far rather be happy than right any day. ~ Douglas Adams

Day 18: Those who are not looking for happiness are the most likely to find it, because those who are searching forget that the surest way to be happy is to seek the happiness of others. ~ Martin Luther King Jr.

Day 19: The greater part of our happiness or misery depends on our dispositions, and not our circumstances. ~ Martha Washington

Day 20: Love is that condition in which the happiness of another person is essential to your own. ~ Robert A. Heinlein

Day 21: I've always thought people would find more pleasure in their routines if they would burst into song at significant moments. ~ John Barrowman

Day 22: All who would win must share it—happiness was born a twin. ~ George Gordon Byron

Day 23: A quiet secluded life in the country, with the possibility of being useful to people to whom it is easy to do good, and who are not accustomed to have it done to them; then work which one hopes may be some use; then rest, nature, books, music, love for one's neighbor—such is my happiness. ~ Leo Tolstoy

Day 24: Whoever is happy will make others happy. ~ Ann Frank

Day 25: Everyone wants to live on top of the mountain, but all the happiness and growth occurs while you're climbing it. ~ Andy Rooney

Day 26: Happiness consists in frequent repetition of pleasure. ~ Arthur Schopenhauer

Day 27: It's a helluva start, being able to recognize what makes you happy. ~ Lucille Ball

Day 28: It was only a sunny smile, and little it cost in the giving, but like morning light it scattered the night and made the day worth living. ~ F. Scott Fitzgerald

Day 29: The more you praise and celebrate your life, the more there is in life to celebrate. ~ Oprah Winfrey

Day 30: Time you enjoy wasting is not wasted time. ~ Martha Troly Curtin

Day 31: Children are happy because they don't have a file in their minds called, 'All the things that could go wrong.' ~ Marianne Williamson

Day 32: The power of finding beauty in the humblest things makes home happy and life lovely. ~ Louisa May Alcott

Day 33: A thing of beauty is a joy forever. ~ John Keats

Day 34: What can I do with my happiness? How can I keep it, conceal it, bury it where I may never lose it? I want to kneel as it falls over me like rain, gather it up with lace and silk, and press it over myself again. ~ Anais Nin

Day 35: Happiness is not a goal…it's a by-product of a life well lived. ~ Eleanor Roosevelt

Day 36: Happiness is not a possession to be prized, it is a quality of thought, a state of mind. ~ Daphne du Maurier

Day 37: I am a happy camper so I guess I'm doing something right. Happiness is like a butterfly; the more you chase it, the more it will elude you, but if you turn your attention to other things, it will come and sit softly on your shoulder. ~ David Thoreau

Day 38: They say a person needs just three things to be truly happy in this world: someone to love, something to do, and something to hope for. ~ Tom Bodett

Day 39: This planet has—or rather had—a problem, which was this: most of the people living on it were unhappy for pretty much of the time. Many solutions were suggested for this problem, but most of these were largely concerned with the movements of small green pieces of paper, which was odd because on the whole it wasn't the small green pieces of paper that were unhappy. ~ Douglas Adams, author of The Hitchhiker's Guide to the Galaxy

Day 40: People are just as happy as they make up their minds to be. ~ Abraham Lincoln

Day 41: After all, what is happiness? Love, they tell me. But love doesn't bring and never has brought happiness. On the contrary, it's a constant state of anxiety, a battlefield; it's sleepless nights, asking ourselves all the time if we're doing the right thing. Real love is composed of ecstasy and agony. ~ Paulo Coelho

Day 42: Be believing, be happy, don't get discouraged. Things will work out. ~ Gordon B. Hinckley

Day 43: I am not proud, but I am happy; and happiness blinds, I think, more than pride. ~ Alexandre Dumas

Day 44: The sense of unhappiness is so much easier to convey than that of happiness. In misery we seem aware of our own egotism: this pain of mine is individual, this nerve that winces belongs to me and to no other. But happiness annihilates us: we lose our identity. ~ Grahame Greene

Day 45: Those who do not know how to see the precious things in life will never be happy. ~ Alex Flinn

Day 46: No one should ever ask themselves that: why am I unhappy? The question caries within it the virus that will destroy everything. If we ask that question, it means we want to find out what makes us happy. If what makes us happy is different from what we have now, then we must either change once and for all or stay as we are, feeling even more unhappy. ~ Paulo Coelho

Day 47: Happiness is a risk. If you're not a little scared, then you're not doing it right. ~ Sarah Addison.

Day 48: It is sometimes easier to be happy if you don't know everything. ~ Alexander McCall Smith

Day 49: Memory is the happiness of being alone. ~ Louis Lowry

Day 50: It's so hard to forget pain, but it's even harder to remember sweetness. We have no scar to show for happiness. We learn so little from peace. ~ Chuck Palahniuk

Day 51: Right in this moment, I can't even remember what unhappy feels like. ~ Maggie Steifvater

Day 52: Fathers filled the small room. Our laughter kept the feathers in the air. I thought about birds. Could they fly if there wasn't someone, somewhere, laughing? ~ Jonathan Safran Foer

Day 53: My happiness is not the means to any end. It is the end. It is its own goal. It is its own purpose. ~ Ayn Rand

Day 54: Woman is not made to be the admiration of all, but the happiness of one. ~ Edmund Burke

Day 55: Obscurity and a competence—that is the life that is best worth living. ~ Mark Twain

Day 56: You have to participate relentless in the manifestation of your own blessings. ~ Elizabeth Gilbert

Day 57: We all live with the objective of being happy; our lives are all different and yet the same. ~ Anne Frank

Day 58: It is a curious thing, but as one travels the world getting older and older, it appears that happiness is easier to get used to than despair. The second time you have a root beer float, for instance, your happiness at sipping the delicious concoction may not be quite as enormous as when you first had a root beer float, and the twelfth time your happiness may be still less enormous, until root beer floats begin to offer you very little happiness at all, because you have become used to the taste of vanilla ice cream and root beer mixed together. However, the second time you find a thumbtack in your root beer float, your despair is much greater than the first time, when you dismissed the thumbtack as a freak accident rather than part of the scheme of a soda jerk, a phrase which here means "ice cream shop employee who is trying to injure your tongue," and by the twelfth time you find a thumbtack, your despair is even greater still, until you can hardly utter the phrase "root beer float" without bursting into tears. It is almost as if happiness is an acquired taste, like coconut cordial or ceviche, to which you can eventually become accustomed, but despair is something surprising each time you encounter it. ~ Lemony Snicket

Day 59: People tend to think that happiness is a stroke of luck, something that will descend like fine weather if you're fortunate. But happiness is the result of personal effort. You fight for it, strive for it, insist upon it, and sometimes even travel around the world looking for it. You have to participate relentlessly. ~ Elizabeth Gilbert

Day 60: Happiness is when what you think, what you say, and what you do are in harmony. ~ Mahatma Ghandi

Day 61: Maybe happiness didn't have to be about the big, sweeping circumstances, about having everything in your life in place. Maybe it was about stringing together a bunch of small pleasures. Wearing slippers and watching the Miss Universe contest. Eating a brownie with vanilla ice cream. Getting to level seven in Dragon Master and knowing there were twenty more levels to go.

Maybe happiness was just a matter of the little upticks- the traffic signal that said "Walk" the second you go there- and downticks- the itch tag at the back of your collar- that happened to every person in the course of the day. Maybe everybody had the same allotted measure of happiness within each day.

Maybe it didn't matter if you were a world-famous heartthrob or a painful geek. Maybe it didn't matter if your friend was possibly dying.

Maybe you just got through it. Maybe that was all you could ask for. ~ Ann Brashares

Day 62: I believe compassion to be one of the few things we can practice that will bring immediate and long-term happiness to our lives. I'm not talking about the short-term gratification of pleasures like sex, drugs or gambling (though I'm not knocking them), but something that will bring true and lasting happiness. The kind that sticks. ~ Dalai Lama XIV

Day 63: The trouble is that we have a bad habit, encouraged by pendants and sophisticates, of considering happiness as something rather stupid. Only pain is intellectual, only evil interesting. This is the treason of the artist: a refusal to admit the banality of evil and the terrible boredom of pain. ~ Ursula K Le Guin

Day 64: Sometimes life knocks you on your ass…get up, get up, get up!! Happiness is not the absence of problems. It's the ability to deal with them. ~ Steve Maraboli

Day 65: There is some kind of sweet innocence to being human—in not having to be just happy or sad—in the nature of being able to be both broken and whole, at the same time. ~ C. Joybell C.

Day 66: And I can't be running back and forth forever between grief and high delight. ~ J.D. Salinger

Day 67: Action may not always bring happiness, but there is no happiness without action. ~ William James

Day 68: This life is yours. Take the power to choose what you want to do and do it well. Take the power to love what you want in life and love it honestly. Take the power to walk in the forest and be a part of nature. Take the power to control your own life. No one else can do it for you. Take the power to make your life happy. ~ Susan Polis SChutz

Day 69: There you go...let it all slide out. Unhappiness can't stick in a person's soul when it's slick with tears. ~ Shannon Hale

Day 70: Seven Deadly Sins
Wealth without work
Pleasure without conscience
Science without humanity
Knowledge without character
Politics without principle
Commerce without morality
Worship without sacrifice.
~ Mahatma Ghandi

Day 71: Love is too precious to be ashamed of. Laurell K. Hamilton

Day 72: Happiness is a perfume you cannot pour on others without getting some on yourself. ~ Ralph Waldo Emerson

Day 73: Happiness. Simple as glass of chocolate or tortuous as the heart. Bitter. Sweet. Alive. ~ Joanne Harris

Day 74: Only the development of compassion and understanding for others can bring us the tranquility and happiness we all seek. ~ Dalai Lama XIV

Day 75: She had never imagined she had the power to make someone else so happy. And not a magical power, either—a purely human one. ~ Cassandra Clare

Day 76: All I ask is one thing, and I'm asking this particularly of young people: please don't be cynical. I hate cynicism, for the record, it's my least favorite quality and it doesn't lead anywhere. Nobody in life gets exactly what they thought they were going to get. But if you work really hard and you're kind, amazing things will happen. ~ Conan O'Brien

Day 77: Expectations make people miserable, so whatever yours are, lower them. You'll definitely be happier. ~ Simon Elkeles

Day 78: I don't know what good it is to know so much and be smart as whips and all if it doesn't make you happy. ~ J.D. Salinger

Day 79: You can't be brave if you've only had wonderful things happen to you. ~ Mary Tyler Moore

Day 80: Happiness in intelligent people is the rarest thing I know. ~ Ernest Hemingway

Day 81: To be stupid, and selfish, and to have good health are the three requirements for happiness—though if stupidity is lacking, the others are useless. ~ Julian Barnes

Day 82: One is happy as a result of one's efforts once one knows the necessary ingredients of happiness: simple tastes, a certain degree of courage, self-denial to a point, love of work, and above all, a clear conscience. ~ George Sand

Day 83: There are random moments - tossing a salad, coming up the driveway to the house, ironing the seams flat on a quilt square, standing at the kitchen window and looking out at the delphiniums, hearing a burst of laughter from one of my children's rooms - when I feel a wavelike rush of joy. This is my true religion: arbitrary moments of nearly painful happiness for a life I feel privileged to lead. ~ Elizabeth Berg

Day 84: The secret of happiness is not in doing what one likes, but in liking what one does. ~ J.M. Barrie

Day 85: Pierre was right when he said that one must believe in the possibility of happiness in order to be happy, and I now believe in it. Let the dead bury the dead, but while I'm alive, I must live and be happy. ~ Leo Tolstoy

Day 86: Until you make peace with who you are, you'll never be content with what you have. ~ Doris Mortman

Day 87: I keep remembering one of my Guru's teachings about happiness. She says that people universally tend to think that happiness is a stroke of luck, something that will maybe descend upon you like fine weather if you're fortunate enough. But that's not how happiness works. Happiness is the consequence of personal effort. You fight for it, strive for it, insist upon it, and sometimes even travel around the world looking for it. You have to participate relentlessly in the manifestations of your own blessings. And once you have achieved a state of happiness, you must never become lax about maintaining it, you must make a mighty effort to keep swimming upward into that happiness forever, to stay afloat on top of it. If you don't you will eat away your innate contentment. It's easy enough to pray when you're in distress but continuing to pray even when your crisis has passed is like a sealing process, helping your soul hold tight to its good attainments. ~ Elizabeth Gilbert from Eat, Pray, Love

Day 88: You don't ask people with knives in their stomachs what would make them happy; happiness is no longer the point. It's all about survival; it's all about whether you pull the knife out and bleed to death or keep it in... ~ Nick Hornby

Day 89: Dustfinger still clearly remembered the feeling of being in love for the first time. How vulnerable his heart had suddenly been! Such a trembling, quivering thing, happy and miserably unhappy at once. ~ Cornelia Funke

Day 90: You will never be happy if you continue to search for happiness. You will never live if you are looking for the meaning of life. ~ Albert Camus

Day 91: A large income is the best recipe for happiness I ever heard of. ~ Jane Austen

Day 92: Keep your best wishes close to your heart and watch what happens. ~ Tony DeLiso

Day 93: ~ The pain I feel now is the happiness I had before. That's the deal. ~ C.S. Lewis

Day 94: Happy girls are the prettiest. ~ Audrey Hepburn

Day 95: There is no happiness like that of being loved by your fellow creatures, and feeling that your presence is an addition to their comfort. ~ Charlotte Bronte

Day 96: Happiness. It was the place where passion, with all its dazzle and drumbeat, met something softer: homecoming and safety and pure sunbeam comfort. It was all those things, intertwined with the heat and the thrill, and it was as bright within her as a swallowed star. ~ Laini Taylor

Day 97: Happiness is the settling of the soul into its most appropriate spot. ~ Aristotle

Day 98: Many people think excitement is happiness…But when you are excited you are not peaceful. True happiness is based on peace. Thich Nhat Hanh

Day 99: We're all golden sunflowers inside. ~ Allen Ginsberg

Day 100: Don't cry because it's over. Smile because it happened. ~ Dr. Seuss

Day 101: Happiness, you see, its just an illusion of Fate, a heavenly sleight of hand designed to make you believe in fairy tales. But there's no happily ever after. You'll find happy endings in books. Some books. ~ Ellen Hopkins

Day 102: Later she remembered all the hours of the afternoon as happy -- one of those uneventful times that seem at the moment only a link between past and future pleasure, but turn out to have been the pleasure itself. ~ F. Scott Fitzgerald

Day 103: Plant seeds of happiness, hope, success, and love; it will all come back to you in abundance. This is the law of nature. ~ Steve Maraboli

Day 104: Happiness is not achieved by the conscious pursuit of happiness; it is generally the by-product of other activities. ~ Aldous Huxley

Day 105: It is an illusion that youth is happy, an illusion of those who have lost it; but the young know they are wretched for they are full of the truthless ideal which have been instilled into them, and each time they come in contact with the real, they are bruised and wounded. It looks as if they were victims of a conspiracy; for the books they read, ideal by the necessity of selection, and the conversation of their elders, who look back upon the past through a rosy haze of forgetfulness, prepare them for an unreal life. They must discover for themselves that all they have read and all they have been told are lies, lies, lies; and each discovery is another nail driven into the body on the cross of life. ~ W. Somerset Maugham

Day 106: Because children grow up, we think a child's purpose is to grow up. But a child's purpose is to be a child. Nature doesn't disdain what lives only for a day. It pours the whole of itself into the each moment. We don't value the lily less for not being made of flint and built to last. Life's bounty is in its flow, later is too late. Where is the song when it's been sung? The dance when it's been danced? It's only we humans who want to own the future, too. We persuade ourselves that the universe is modestly employed in unfolding our destination. We note the haphazard chaos of history by the day, by the hour, but there is something wrong with the picture. Where is the unity, the meaning, of nature's highest creation? Surely those millions of little streams of accident and wilfulness have their correction in the vast underground river which, without a doubt, is carrying us to the place where we're expected! But there is no such place, that's why it's called utopia. The death of a child has no more meaning than the death of armies, of nations. Was the child happy while he lived? That is a proper question, the only question. If we can't arrange our own happiness, it's a conceit beyond vulgarity to arrange the happiness of those who come after us. ~ Tom Stoppard

Day 107: We buy things we don't need with money we don't have to impress people we don't like. ~ Dave Ramsey

Day 108: There is only one way to happiness and that is to cease worrying about things which are beyond the power or our will. ~ Epictetus

Day 109: The trick is in what one emphasizes. We either make ourselves miserable, or we make ourselves happy. The amount of work is the same. ~ Carlos Castaneda

Day 110: Count your age by friends, not years. Count your life by smiles, not tears. ~ John Lennon

Day 111: Growing old is mandatory. Growing up is optional. ~ Carroll Bryant

Day 112: The reason people find it so hard to be happy is that they always see the past better than it was, the present worse than it is, and the future less resolved than it will be. ~ Marcel Pagnol

Day 113: Age does not make us childish, as some may say; it finds us true children. ~ Johann Wolfgang von Goethe

Day 114: If you wish to be happy,Eragon, Think not of what is to come nor of that which you have no control over but rather of the now and that which you are able to change. ~ Christopher Paolini

Day 115: Ahhh. Bed, book, kitten, sandwich. All one needed in life, really. ~ Jacqueline Kelly

Day 116: I do not think we have a "right" to happiness. If happiness happens, say thanks. ~ Marlene Dietrich

Day 117: As I focus on diligent joy, I also keep remembering a simple idea my friend Darcey told me once -- that all the sorrow and trouble of this world is caused by unhappy people. Not only in the big global Hitler-'n'-Stalin picture, but also on the smallest personal level. Even in my own life, I can see exactly where my episodes of unhappiness have brought suffering or distress or (at the very least) inconvenience to those around me. The search for contentment is, therefore, not merely a self-preserving and self-benefiting act, but also a generous gift to the world. Clearing out all your misery gets you out of the way. You cease being an obstacle, not only to yourself but to anyone else. Only then are you free to serve and enjoy other people. ~ Elizabeth Gilbert

Day 118: Happiness is excitement that has found a settling down place, but there is always a little corner flapping around. ~ E.L. Konigsburg

Day 119: All happiness depends on courage and work. ~ Honore De Balzac

Day 120: Happiness is a warm puppy. ~ Charles M. Schulz

Day 121: Part of the problem with the word 'disabilities' is that it immediately suggests an inability to see or hear or walk or do other things that many of us take for granted. But what of people who can't feel? Or talk about their feelings? Or manage their feelings in constructive ways? What of people who aren't able to form close and strong relationships? And people who cannot find fulfillment in their lives, or those who have lost hope, who live in disappointment and bitterness and find in life no joy, no love? These, it seems to me, are the real disabilities. ~ Fred Rogers

Day 122: True happiness is to enjoy the present, without anxious dependence upon the future, not to amuse ourselves with either hopes or fears but to rest satisfied with what we have, which is sufficient, for he that is so wants nothing. The greatest blessings of mankind are within us and within our reach. A wise man is content with his lot, whatever it may be, without wishing for what he has not. ~ Lucius Annaeus Seneca

Day 123: Even if things don't unfold the way you expected, don't be disheartened or give up. One who continues to advance will win in the end. ~ Daisaku Ikeda

Day 124: Don't aim at success. The more you aim at it and make it a target, the more you are going to miss it. For success, like happiness, cannot be pursued; it must ensue, and it only does so as the unintended side effect of one's personal dedication to a cause greater than oneself or as the by-product of one's surrender to a person other than oneself. Happiness must happen, and the same holds for success: you have to let it happen by not caring about it. I want you to listen to what your conscience commands you to do and go on to carry it out to the best of your knowledge. Then you will live to see that in the long-run— in the long-run, I say!—success will follow you precisely because you had forgotten to think about it. ~ Viktor E. Frankl

Day 125: Very little is needed to make a happy life; it is all within yourself in your way of thinking. ~ Marcus Aurelius

Day 126: Sometimes you break your heart in the right way, if you know what I mean. ~ Gregory David Roberts

Day 127: Always forgive, but never forget, else you will be a prisoner of your own hatred, and doomed to repeat your mistakes forever. ~ Wil Zeus

Day 128: What sunshine is to flowers, smiles are to humanity. These are but trifles, to be sure; but scattered along life's pathway, the good they do is inconceivable. ~ Joseph Addison

Day 129: There is a kind of happiness and wonder that makes you serious. It is too good to waste on jokes. ~ C.S. Lewis

Day 130: The most important thing is to enjoy your life—to be happy---that's all that matters. ~ Audrey Hepburn

Day 131: Happiness does not come from without. It comes from within. ~ Helen Keller

Day 132: Seize the moments of happiness, love and be loved! That is the only reality in the world, all else is folly. It is the one thing we are interested in here. ~ Leo Tolstoy

Day 133: Happiness is like those palaces in fairytales whose gates are guarded by dragons: We must fight in order to conquer it. ~ Alexandre Dumas

Day 134: The purpose of government is to enable the people of a nation to live in safety and happiness. Government exists for the interests of the governed, not for the governors. ~ Thomas Jefferson

Day 135: I am still determined to be cheerful and happy, in whatever situation I may be; for I have also learned from experience that the greater part of our happiness or misery depends upon our dispositions, and not upon our circumstances. ~ Martha Washington

Day 136: And lastly from that period I remember riding in a taxi one afternoon between very tall buildings under a mauve and rosy sky; I began to bawl because I had everything I wanted and knew I would never be so happy again. ~ F. Scott Fitzgerald

Day 137: Happiness lies within the joy of achievement and the joy of creative effort ~ Franklin D. Roosevelt

Day 138: It was their secret, a secret meant for just the two of them, and she'd never been able to imagine how it would sound coming from someone else. But, somehow, Logan made it sound just right. ~ Nicholas Sparks

Day 139: The way I define happiness is being the creator of your experience, choosing to take pleasure in what you have, right now, regardless of the circumstances, while being the best you that you can be. ~ Leo Babauta

Day 140: Happiness is having a large, loving, caring, close-knit family in another city. George Burns

Day 141: ...is ignorance bliss, I don't know, but it's so painful to think, and tell me, what did thinking ever do for me, to what great place did thinking ever bring me? I think and think and think, I've thought myself out of happiness one million times, but never once into it. ~ Jonathan Safran Foer

Day 142: Hurt is a part of life. To be honest, I think hurt is a part of happiness, that our definition of happiness has gotten very narrow lately, very nervous, a little afraid of this brawling, fabulous, unpredictable world. ~ Julian Gough

Day 143: The belief that unhappiness is selfless and happiness is selfish is misguided. It's more selfless to act happy. It takes energy, generosity, and discipline to be unfailingly lighthearted, yet everyone takes the happy person for granted. No one is careful of his feelings or tries to keep his spirits high. He seems self-sufficient; he becomes a cushion for others. And because happiness seems unforced, that person usually gets no credit. ~ Gretchen Rubin

Day 144: I am intrigued by the smile upon your face, and the sadness within your eyes. ~ Jeremy Aldana

Day 145: Wealth consists not in having great possessions, but in having few wants. ~ Epictetus

Day 146: I had rather hear my dog bark at a crow, than a man swear he loves me. ~ William Shakespeare, Much Ado About Nothing

Day 147: Money may not buy happiness, but I'd rather cry in a Jaguar than on a bus. ~ Francois Sagan

Day 148: One swallow does not make a summer, neither does one fine day; similarly one day or brief time of happiness does not make a person entirely happy. ~ Aristotle

Day 149: The foolish man seeks happiness in the distance. The wise grows it under his feet. ~ James Oppenheim

Day 150: There's nothing like deep breaths after laughing that hard. Nothing in the world like a sore stomach for the right reasons. ~ Stephen Cbosky

Day 151: If you have any young friends who aspire to become writers, the second greatest favor you can do them is to present them with copies of The Elements of Style.

The first greatest, of course, is to shoot them now, while they're happy. ~ Dorothy Parker

Day 152: A happy person is not a person in a certain set of circumstances, but rather a person with a certain set of attitudes. ~ Hugh Downs

Day 153: Happiness is a choice that requires effort at times. Aeschylus

Day 154: My happiness grows in direct proportion to my acceptance, and in inverse proportion to my expectations." ~ Michael J. Fox

Day 155: It isn't what you have, or who you are, or where you are, or what you are doing that makes you happy or unhappy. It is what you think about. ~ Dale Carnegie

Day 156: In the end, the number of prayers we say may contribute to our happiness, but the number of prayers we answer may be of even greater importance. ~ Dieter F. Uchtdorf

Day 157: It's funny how one summer can change everything. It must be something about the heat and the smell of chlorine, fresh-cut grass and honeysuckle, asphalt sizzling after late-day thunderstorms, the steam rising while everything drips around it. Something about long, lazy days and whirring air conditioners and bright plastic flip-flops from the drugstore thwacking down the street. Something about fall being so close, another year, another Christmas, another beginning. So much in one summer, stirring up like the storms that crest at the end of each day, blowing out all the heat and dirt to leave everything gasping and cool. Everyone can reach back to one summer and lay a finger to it, finding the exact point when everything changed. That summer was mine. ~ Sarah Dessen

Day 158: Happiness and the absurd are two sons of the same earth. They are inseparable. ~ Albert Camus

Day 159: Happiness doesn't lie in conspicuous consumption and the relentless amassing of useless crap. Happiness lies in the person sitting beside you and your ability to talk to them. Happiness is clear-headed human interaction and empathy. Happiness is home. And home is not a house-home is a mythological conceit. It is a state of mind. A place of communion and unconditional love. It is where, when you cross its threshold, you finally feel at peace. ~ Dennis Lehane

Day 160: You cannot protect yourself from sadness without protecting yourself from happiness. ~ Jonathan Safran Foer

Day 161: That's the secret to life... replace one worry with another.... ~ Charles M. Schulz

Day 162: To be stupid, selfish, and have good health are three requirements for happiness, though if stupidity is lacking, all is lost. ~ Gustave Flaubert

Day 163: You have everything you need for complete peace and total happiness right now. ~ Wayne W. Dyer

Day 164: It is almost as if happiness is an acquired taste, like coconut cordial or ceviche, to which you can eventually become accustomed, but despair is something surprising each time you encounter it. ~ Lemony Snicket

Day 165: I am not good at noticing I am happy except in retrospect. ~ Tana French

Day 166: Why? Why does what was beautiful suddenly shatter in hindsight because it concealed dark truths? Why does the memory of years of happy marriage turn to gall when our partner is revealed to have had a lover all those years? Because such a situation makes it impossible to be happy? But we were happy! Sometimes the memory of happiness cannot stay true because it ended unhappily. Because happiness is only real if it lasts forever? Because things always end painfully if they contained pain, conscious or unconscious, all along? But what is unconscious, unrecognized pain? ~ Bernhard Schlink

Day 167: Come clean with a child heart
Laugh as peaches in the summer wind
Let rain on a house roof be a song
Let the writing on your face
be a smell of apple orchards on late June.
~ Carl Sandburg

Day 168: Sadness gives depth. Happiness gives height. Sadness gives roots. Happiness gives branches. Happiness is like a tree going into the sky, and sadness is like the roots going down into the womb of the earth. Both are needed, and the higher a tree goes, the deeper it goes, simultaneously. The bigger the tree, the bigger will be its roots. In fact, it is always in proportion. That's its balance. ~ Osho

Day 169: People wait around too long for love. I'm happy with all of my lusts! ~ C. Joybell C.

Day 170: The only way to find true happiness is to risk being completely cut open. ~ Chuck Palahnuik

Day 171: ...nothing wonderful lasted forever. Joy was as fleeting as a shooting star that crossed the evening sky, ready to blink out at any moment. ~ Nicholas Sparks

Day 172: ~ Happiness doesn't result from what we get, but from what we give. ~ Ben Carson

Day 173: There is no beauty in sadness. No honor in suffering. No growth in fear. No relief in hate. It's just a waste of perfectly good happiness. ~ Katerina Stoykova Klemer

Day 174: I like to believe that you don't need to reach a certain goal to be happy. I prefer to think that happiness is always there, and that when things don't go the way we might like them to, it's a sign from above that something even better is right around the corner. ~ David Archuleta

Day 175: I consider myself a stained-glass window. And this is how I live my life. Closing no doors and covering no windows; I am the multi-colored glass with light filtering through me, in many different shades. Allowing light to shed and fall into many many hues. My job is not to direct anything, but only to filter into many colors. My answer is destiny and my guide is joy. And there you have me. ~ C. Joybell C.

Day 176: Happiness comes from within. It is not dependent on external things or on other people. You become vulnerable and can be easily hurt when your feelings of security and happiness depend on the behavior and actions of other people. Never give your power to anyone else. ~ Brian L. Weiss

Day 177: You can't buy happiness. ~ Kurt Cobain

Day 178: He whose face gives no light, shall never become a star. ~ William Blake

Day 179: I needed to stop being what everyone thought I was. ~ Sarah Addison Allen

Day 180: Of all forms of caution, caution in love is perhaps the most fatal to true happiness. ~ Bertrand Russell

Day 181: Laughter is more than just a pleasurable activity...When people laugh together, they tend to talk and touch more and to make eye contact more frequently. ~ Gretchin Rubin

Day 182: Human happiness and moral duty are inseparably connected. ~ George Washington

Day 183: Happiness is a state of activity. ~ Aristotle

Day 184: If you deliberately set out to be less than you are capable, you'll be unhappy for the rest of your life. ~ Abraham Harold Maslow

Day 185: Happiness is not in the mere possession of money; it lies in the joy of achievement, in the thrill of creative effort. ~ Franklin D. Roosevelt

Day 186: I don't know what your destiny will be, but one thing I know: the only ones among you who will be really happy are those who have sought and found how to serve. ~ Albert Schweitzer

Day 187: Of all the means to insure happiness throughout the whole life, by far the most important is the acquisition of friends. ~ Epicurus

Day 188: I'm a happy person. If you want to be around me, you can either choose to be happy too, or follow the signs to the nearest exit! ~ Sharon Swan

Day 189: You can have it all. Just not all at once. ~ Oprah Winfrey

Day 190: If more of us valued food and cheer and song above hoarded gold, it would be a merrier world. ~ J.R.R. Tolkien

Day 191: Self-esteem comes from being able to define the world in your own terms and refusing to abide by the judgments of others. ~ Oprah Winfrey

Day 192: Of all the means to insure happiness through the whole life, by far the most important is the acquisition of friends. ~ Epicurus

Day 193: The best thing about dreams is that fleeting moment, when you are between asleep and awake, when you don't know the difference between reality and fantasy, when for just that one moment you feel with your entire soul that the dream is reality, and it really happened. ~ Oprah Winfrey

Day 194: The earth was warm under me, and warm as I crumbled it through my fingers, I kept as still as I could. Nothing happened. I did not expect anything to happen. I was something that lay under the sun and felt it, like the pumpkins, and I did not want to be anything more. I was entirely happy. Perhaps we feel like that when we die and become a part of something entire, whether it is sun and air, or goodness and knowledge. At any rate, that is happiness;

to be dissolved into something complete and great. When it comes to one, it comes as naturally as sleep. ~ Willa Cather

Day 195: Turn your wounds into wisdom. ~ Oprah Winfrey

Day 196: I am a happy person. If you want to be around me, you can either be happy too, or follow the signs to the nearest exit! ~ Sharon Swan

Day 197: Why not let people differ about their answers to the great mysteries of the Universe? Let each seek one's own way to the highest, to one's own sense of supreme loyalty in life, one's ideal of life. Let each philosophy, each world-view bring forth its truth and beauty to a larger perspective, that people may grow in vision, stature and dedication. ~ Algernon Blackwood

Day 198: Letting go means to come to the realization that some people are a part of your history, but not a part of your destiny. ~ Steve Maraboli

Day 199: Some women have a weakness for shoes…I can go barefoot if necessary. I have a weakness for books. ~ Oprah Winfrey

Day 200: I've got nothing to do today but smile. ~ Paul Simon

Day 201: As you become more clear about who you really are, you'll be better able to decide what is best for you—the first time around. ~ Oprah Winfrey

Day 202: Cry. Forgive. Learn. Move on. Let your tears water the seeds of your future happiness. ~ Steve Maraboli

Day 203: It takes three to make love, not two: you, your spouse, and God. Without God people only succeed in bringing out the worst in one another. Lovers who have nothing else to do but love each other soon find there is nothing else. Without a central loyalty life is unfinished. ~ Fulton J. Sheen

Day 204: For those who are poor in happiness, each time is a first time; happiness never becomes a habit. ~ Marilyn Monroe

Day 205: The biggest adventure you can ever take is to live the life of your dreams. ~ Oprah Winfrey

Day 206: Destiny is real. And she's not mild-mannered. She will come around and hit you in the face and knock you over and before you know what hit you, you're naked-stripped of everything you thought you knew and everything you thought you didn't know- and there you are! A bloody nose, bruises all over you, and naked. And it's the most beautiful thing. ~ C. Joybell C.

Day 207: Maybe you think you'll be entitled to more happiness later by forgoing all of it now, but it doesn't work that way. Happiness takes as much practice as unhappiness does. It's by living that you live more. By waiting you wait more. Every waiting day makes your life a little less. Every lonely day makes you a little smaller. Every day you put off your life makes you less capable of living it. ~ Ann Brashares

Day 208: I never did anything according to what anyone else wanted. That's why I think I am happy. I do everything 100%--even my stupidest missteps. I know when I'm getting ready to mess up, I'm going to do it full-on. That's the way I was as a kid. Even into adulthood, I look back at some things and go, 'I can't believe I did that.' But I can also go back and say, 'I did that, I know I'm responsible for that, and I can make amends,' and we can all laugh at it, because it's my mistake. I try not to blame it on anyone else unless I fully know it was their fault--and then I have no problem pointing the finger. ~ Sandra Bullock

Day 209: We can't become what we need to be by remaining what we are. ~ Oprah Winfey

Day 210: Let us be grateful to the people who make us happy; they are the charming gardeners who make our souls blossom. ~ Marcel Proust

Day 211: Meditate. Breathe consciously. Listen. Pay attention. Treasure every moment. Make the connection. ~ Oprah Winfrey

Day 212: Be happy with who you are, and you can do anything you want. ~ Steve Maraboli

Day 213: Life is painful. It has thorns, like the stem of a rose. Culture and art are the roses that bloom on the stem. The flower is yourself, your humanity. Art is the liberation of the humanity inside yourself. ~ Daisaku Ikeda

Day 214: Happiness is a gift and the trick is not to expect it, but to delight in it when it comes. ~ Charles Dickens

Day 215: Everyone wants to ride with you in the limo, but what you want is someone who will take the bus with you when the limo breaks down. ~ Oprah Winfrey

Day 216: Perfect love casts out fear. Where there is love there are no demands, no expectations, no dependency. I do not demand that you make me happy; my happiness does not lie in you. If you were to leave me, I will not feel sorry for myself; I enjoy your company immensely, but I do not cling. ~ Anthony de Mello

Day 217: With my eyes closed, I would touch a familiar book and draw its fragrance deep inside me. This was enough to make me happy. ~ Haruki Marukami

Day 218: Remember, happiness doesn't depend upon who you are or what you have, it depends solely upon what you think. ~ Dale Carnegie

Day 219: I believe that every single event in life happens in an opportunity to choose lover over fear. ~ Oprah Winfrey

Day 220: Happiness is the consequence of personal effort. You fight for it, strive for it, insist upon it, and sometimes even travel around the world looking for it. You have to participate relentlessly in the manifestations of your own blessings. And once you have achieved a state of happiness, you must never become lax about maintaining it. You must make a mighty effort to keep swimming upward into that happiness forever, to stay afloat on top of it. ~ Elizabeth Gilbert

Day 221: Do the one thing you think you cannot do. Fail at it. Try again. Do better the second time. The only people who never tumble are those who never mount the high wire. ~ Oprah Winfrey

Day 222: Those born to wealth, and who have the means of gratifying every wish, know not what is the real happiness of life, just as those who have been tossed on the stormy waters of the ocean on a few frail planks can alone realize the blessings of fair weather. ~ Alexandre Dumas

Day 223: Can a person steal happiness? Or is just another internal, infernal human trick? ~ Markus Zusak

Day 224: There are a few moments in your life when you are truly and completely happy, and you remember to give thanks. Even as it happens you are nostalgic for the moment, you are tucking it away in your scrapbook. ~ David Benioff

Day 225: Be thankful for what you have; you'll end up having more. If you concentrate on what you don't have, you will never, ever have enough. ~ Oprah Winfrey

Day 226: We've got everything we need right here, and everything we need is enough. ~ Jack Johnson

Day 227: Got no checkbooks, got no banks. Still I'd like to express my thanks - I've got the sun in the mornin' and the moon at night. ~ Irving Berlin

Day 228: No one can grant you happiness. Happiness is a choice we all have the power to make. ~ Dean Koontz

Day 229: Dogs are my favorite role models. I want to work like a dog, doing what I was born to do with joy and purpose. I want to play like a dog, with total, jolly abandon. I want to love like a dog, with unabashed devotion and complete lack of concern about what people do for a living, how much money they have, or how much they weigh. The fact that we still live with dogs, even when we don't have to herd or hunt our dinner, gives me hope for humans and canines alike. ~ Oprah Winfrey

Day 230: Sanity and happiness are an impossible combination. ~ Mark Twain

Day 231: The whole point of being alive is to evolve into the complete person you were intended to be.~ Oprah Winfrey

Day 232: I've pursued dreams and achieved them, but I don't think anybody should think their life is incomplete if they don't follow some dream. Happiness doesn't come from achievements, or money, or any sort of treasure. Happiness is a frame of mind, not a destination. It's appreciating what you've got and building relationships with those around you. ~ Janette Rallison

Day 233: No one asked you to be happy. Get to work. ~ Colette

Day 234: Marriage becomes hard work once you have poured the entirety of your life's expectations for happiness into the hands of one mere person. Keeping that going is hard work. ~ Elizabeth Gilbert

Day 235: I trust that everything happens for a reason, even if we are not wise enough to see it. ~ Oprah Winfrey

Day 236: There is no greater power than that of a laugh and happiness is a force which can save a person from the horrors of the world. ~ Hillary DePiano

Day 237: I have a million things to talk to you about. All I want in this world is you. I want to see you and talk. I want the two of us to begin everything from the beginning. ~ Haruki Murakami

Day 238: You, of all people, deserve a happy ending. Despite everything that happened to you, you aren't bitter. You aren't cold. You've just retreated a little and been shy, and that's okay. If I were a fairy godmother, I would give you your heart's desire in an instant. And I would wipe away your tears and tell you not to cry. ~ Sylvain Reynard

Day 239: Every day brings a chance to live free of regret and with as much joy, fun, and laughter as you can stand. ~ Oprah Winfrey

Day 240: Success is getting what you want, happiness is wanting what you get. ~ W.P. Kinsella

Day 241: The whole point of being alive is to evolve into the compete person you were intended to be. ~ Oprah Winfrey

Day 242: We are not going to change the whole world, but we can change ourselves and feel free as birds. We can be serene even in the midst of calamities and, by our serenity, make others more tranquil. Serenity is contagious. If we smile at someone, he or she will smile back. And a smile costs nothing. We should plague everyone with joy. If we are to die in a minute, why not die happily, laughing? ~ Swami Satchidananda

Day 243: My past hour has not defined me, destroyed me, deterred me, or defeated me; it has only strengthened me. ~ Steve Maraboli

Day 244: Happiness is the most natural thing in the world when you have it, and the slowest, strangest, most impossible thing when you don't. It's like learning a foreign language: You can think about the words all you want, but you'll never be able to speak it until you suck up your courage and say them out loud. ~ Dan Wells

Day 245: Breathe. Let go. And remind yourself that this very moment is the only one you know you have for sure. ~ Oprah Winfrey

Day 246: Sometimes we must undergo hardships, breakups, and narcissistic wounds, which shatter the flattering image that we had of ourselves, in order to discover two truths: that we are not who we thought we were; and that the loss of a cherished pleasure is not necessarily the loss of true happiness and well-being. ~ Jean Yves Leloup

Day 247: I'm going to enjoy every second, and I'm going to know I'm enjoying it while I'm enjoying it. Most people don't live; they just race. They are trying to reach some goal far away on the horizon, and in the heat of the going they get so breathless and panting that they lose sight of the beautiful, tranquil country they are passing through; and then the first thing they know, they are old and worn out, and it doesn't make any difference whether they've reached the goal or not. Jean Webster

Day 248: He was a wonderful man. And when a man is that special, you know it sooner than you think possible. You recognize it instinctively, and you're certain that no matter what happens, there will never be another one like him. ~ Nicholas Sparks

Day 249: Think like a queen. A queen is not afraid to fail. Failure is another stepping stone to greatness. ~ Oprah Winfrey

Day 250: It's been my experience that you can nearly always enjoy things if you make up your mind firmly that you will. ~ L.M. Montgomery

Day 251: The whole point of being alive is to evolve into the complete person you were intended to be. ~ Oprah Winfrey

Day 252: Fate never promises to tell you everything up front. You aren't always shown the path in life you're supposed to take. But if there was one thing she'd learned in the past few weeks, it was that sometimes, when you're really lucky, you meet someone with a map.~ Sarah Addison Allen

Day 253: After all the world is indeed beautiful and if we were any other creature than man we might be continuously happy in it. ~ Sebastian Barry

Day 254: We have no more right to consume happiness without producing it than to consume wealth without producing it. ~ George Bernard Shaw

Day 255: True forgiveness is when you can say, "Thank you for that experience." ~ Oprah Winfrey

Day 256: There's a taste in the air, sweet and vaguely antiseptic, that reminds him of his teenage years in these streets, and of a general state of longing, a hunger for life to begin that from this distance seems like happiness. ~ Ian McEwan

Day 257: Love and compassion are the mother and father of a smile. We need to create more smiles in our world today. Smiles, after all, pave the way to a happy world. ~ Steve Maraboli

Day 258: The truly revolutionary promise of our nation's founding document is the freedom to pursue happiness-with-a-capital-H. ~ Dan Savage

Day 259: Step Away from the Mean Girls...
...and say bye-bye to feeling bad about your looks.
Are you ready to stop colluding with a culture that makes
so many of us feel physically inadequate? Say goodbye to
your inner critic, and take this pledge to be kinder to
yourself and others.

This is a call to arms. A call to be gentle, to be forgiving, to
be generous with yourself. The next time you look into the
mirror, try to let go of the story line that says you're too fat
or too sallow, too ashy or too old, your eyes are too small
or your nose too big; just look into the mirror and see your
face. When the criticism drops away, what you will see
then is just you, without judgment, and that is the first step
toward transforming your experience of the world. ~ Oprah
Winfrey

Day 260: Happiness quite unshared can scarcely be called
happiness; it has no taste. ~ Charlotte Bronte

Day 261: It makes no difference how many peaks you
reach if there was no pleasure in the climb. ~ Oprah
Winfrey

Day 262: There is nothing more rare, nor more beautiful,
than a woman being unapologetically herself; comfortable
in her perfect imperfection. To me, that is the true essence
of beauty. ~ Steve Maraboli

Day 263: Letting go gives us freedom, and freedom is the
only condition for happiness. If, in our heart, we still cling
to anything - anger, anxiety, or possessions - we cannot be
free. ~ Thich Nhat Hanh

Day 264: I shall take the heart. For brains do not make one happy, and happiness is the best thing in the world ~ L. Frank Baum

Day 265: Surround yourself only with people who are going to take you higher. ~ Oprah Winfrey

Day 266: You must be the best judge of your own happiness. ~ Jane Austen

Day 267: Are you going to allow the world around you to change while you remain stagnant? Make this the time you throw away old habits that have hindered your happiness and success and finally allow your greatest self to flourish. ~ Steve Maraboli

Day 268: The great source of both the misery and disorders of human life, seems to arise from over-rating the difference between one permanent situation and another. Avarice over-rates the difference between poverty and riches: ambition, that between a private and a public station: vain-glory, that between obscurity and extensive reputation. The person under the influence of any of those extravagant passions, is not only miserable in his actual situation, but is often disposed to disturb the peace of society, in order to arrive at that which he so foolishly admires. The slightest observation, however, might satisfy him, that, in all the ordinary situations of human life, a well-disposed mind may be equally calm, equally cheerful, and equally contented. Some of those situations may, no doubt, deserve to be preferred to others: but none of them can deserve to be pursued with that passionate ardor which drives us to violate the rules either of prudence or of justice; or to corrupt the future tranquility of our minds, either by shame from the remembrance of our own folly, or by remorse from the horror of our own injustice. ~ Adam Smith

Day 269: When you undervalue what you do, the world will undervalue who you are. ~ Oprah Winfrey

Day 270: No medicine cures what happiness cannot. ~ Gabriel Garcia Marquez

Day 271: Only make decisions that support your self-image, self-esteem, and self-worth. ~ Oprah Winfrey

Day 272: Can you be happy with the movies, and the ads, and the clothes in the stores, and the doctors, and the eyes as you walk down the street all telling you there is something wrong with you? No. You cannot be happy. Because, you poor darling baby, you believe them. ~ Katherine Dunn

Day 273: The trick. . .is to find the balance between the bright colors of humor and the serious issues of identity, self-loathing, and the possibility for intimacy and love when it seems no longer possible or, sadder yet, no longer necessary. ~ Wendy Wasserstien

Day 274: They say all marriages are made in heaven, but so are thunder and lightning. ~ Clint Eastwood

Day 275: Real integrity is doing the right thing, knowing that nobody's going to know whether you did it or not. ~ Oprah Winfrey

Day 276: Create all the happiness you are able to create; remove all the misery you are able to remove. ~ Jeremy Bentham

Day 277: Non-violence, which is the quality of the heart, cannot come by an appeal to the brain. ~ Mahatma Ghandhi

Day 278: Indeed there has never been any explanation of the ebb and flow in our veins--of happiness and unhappiness. ~ Virginia Woolf

Day 279: Challenges are gifts that force us to search for a new center of gravity. Don't fight them. Just find a new way to stand. ~ Oprah Winfrey

Day 280: Isn't what you have or who you are or where you are or what you are doing that makes you happy or unhappy. It is what you think about it. ~ Dale Carnegie

Day 281: I know for sure that what we dwell on is who we become. ~ Oprah Winfrey

Day 282: The summit of happiness is reached when a person is ready to be what he is. ~ Desiderius Erasmus Roterordamus

Day 283: Surely every one realizes, at some point along the way, that he is capable of living a far better life than the one he has chosen. ~ Henry Miller

Day 284: It does not matter how long you are spending on the earth, how much money you have gathered or how much attention you have received. It is the amount of positive vibration you have radiated in life that matters. ~ Amit Ray

Day 285: One of the hardest things in life to learn are which bridges to cross and which bridges to burn. ~ Oprah Winfrey

Day 286: It seemed like this day could go in so many directions, like a spiderweb shooting out toward endless possibilities. Whenever you made a choice, especially one you'd been resisting, it always affected everything else, some in big ways, like a tremor beneath your feet, others in so tiny a shift you hardly noticed a change at all. But it was happening. ~ Sarah Dessen

Day 287: If you're not happy in life then you need to change, calibrate, readjust...flush your negative energy and fill it with positive energy; How do we do that you might ask? well I would start by making others happy, deseases are not the only thing that spreads easy. We are all connected in some form of unseen energy... think how those around you will impact you and make you feel if they were happy? ~ Al Munoz

Day 288: To be happy—one must find bliss. ~ Gloria Vanderbilt

Day 289: Your true passion should feel like breathing; it's that natural. ~ Oprah Winfrey

Day 290: You can't be happy unless you are unhappy sometimes. ~ Lauren Oliver

Day 291: When I look at the future, it's so bright it burns my eyes! ~ Oprah Winfrey

Day 292: Money can't buy happiness, but it certainly is a stress reliever. ~ Besa Kosova

Day 293: Actually, I jade very quickly. Once is usually enough. Either once only, or every day. If you do something once it's exciting, and if you do it every day it's exciting. But if you do it, say, twice or just almost every day, it's not good any more. ~ Andy Warhol

Day 294: What is more cheerful, now, in the fall of the year, than an open-wood-fire? Do you hear those little chirps and twitters coming out of that piece of apple-wood? Those are the ghosts of the robins and blue-birds that sang upon the bough when it was in blossom last Spring. In Summer whole flocks of them come fluttering about the fruit-trees under the window: so I have singing birds all the year round. ~ Thomas Bailey Aldrich

Day 295: You get in life what you have the courage to ask for. ~ Oprah Winfrey

Day 296: An ordinary man can surround himself with two thousand books and thenceforward have at least one place in the world in which it is always possible to be happy. ~ Augustine Birrell

Day 297: Laughter is poison to fear. ~ George R. R. Martin

Day 298: Leave behind the passive dreaming of a rose-tinted future. The energy of happiness exists in living today with roots sunk firmly in reality's soil. ~ Daisaku Ikeda

Day 299: Cheers to a new year and another chance for us to get it right. ~ Oprah Winfrey

Day 300: Rules for happiness: Something to do, someone to love, something to hope for. ~ Immanuel Kant

Day 301: Doing the best at this moment puts you in the best place for the next moment! ~ Oprah Winfrey

Day 302: If you're going to binge, literature is definitely the way to do it. ~ Oprah Winfrey

Day 303: You are built not to shrink down to less but to blossom into more. ~ Oprah Winfrey

Day 304: So go ahead. Fall down. The world looks different from the ground. ~ Oprah Winfrey

Day 305: I've come to believe that each of us has a personal calling that's as unique as a fingerprint - and that the best way to succeed is to discover what you love and then find a way to offer it to others in the form of service, working hard, and also allowing the energy of the universe to lead you. ~ Oprah Winfrey

Day 306: Whatever you fear most has no power—it is your fear that has the power. ~ Oprah Winfrey

Day 307: I finally realized that being grateful to my body was key to giving love to myself. ~ Oprah Winfrey

Day 308: I've learned not to worry about what might come next. ~ Oprah Winfrey

Day 309: You don't become what you want, you become what you believe. ~ Oprah Winfrey

Day 310: Learn to value yourself, which means: fight for your happiness. ~ Ayn Rand

Day 311: You are responsible for your life. You can't keep blaming somebody else for your dysfunction. Life is really about moving on. ~ Oprah Winfrey

Day 312: I finally realized that being grateful to my body was key to giving more love to myself. ~ Oprah Winfrey

Day 313: I've learned not to worry about what might come next. ~ Oprah Winfrey

Day 314: It doesn't matter who you are, where you come from. The ability to triumph begins with you—always. ~ Oprah Winfrey

Day 315: If a man wants you, nothing can keep him away. If he doesn't want you, nothing can make him stay. ~ Oprah Winfrey

Day 316: I don't want anyone who doesn't want me. ~ Oprah Winfrey

Day 317: ~ The best of times are now. ~ Oprah Winfrey

Day 318: With every experience, you alone are painting your own canvas, thought by thought, choice by choice. ~ Oprah Winfrey

Day 319: Every day brings a chance for you to draw in a breath, kick off your shoes, and dance. ~ Oprah Winfrey

Day 320: The best way to cheer yourself is to try to cheer someone else up. ~Mark Twain

Day 321: Follow your instincts. That's where true wisdom manifests itself. ~ Oprah Winfrey

Day 322: Education is the key to unlocking the world, a passport to freedom. ~ Oprah Winfrey

Day 323: You are where you are in life because of what you believe is possible for yourself. ~ Oprah Winfrey

Day 324: I am grateful for the blessings of wealth, but it hasn't changed who I am. My feet are still on the ground. I'm just wearing better shoes. ~ Oprah Winfrey

Day 325: You get to know who you really are in a crisis. ~ Oprah Winfrey

Day 326: Luck is a matter of preparation meeting opportunity. ~ Oprah Winfrey

Day 327: Your calling isn't something that somebody can tell you about. It's what you feel. It is the thing that gives you juice. The thing that you are supposed to do. And nobody can tell you what that is. ~ Oprah Winfrey

Day 328: You aren't your past, you are probability of your future. ~ Oprah Winfrey

Day 329: To love yourself is a never-ending journey. ~ Oprah Winfrey

Day 330: I think and think and think, I've thought myself out of happiness one million times but never once into it. ~ Jonathon Safran Foer

Day 331: If you want your life to be more rewarding, you have to change the way you think. ~ Oprah Winfrey

Day 332: If friends disappoint you over and over, that's in large part your own fault. Once someone has shown a tendency to be self-centered, you need to recognize that and take care of yourself; people aren't going to change simply because you want them to. ~ Oprah Winfrey

Day 333: You cannot be with someone just because you don't want to hurt him. You have your own happiness to think about.~ Melissa De la Cruz

Day 334: I'm kind of a paranoiac in reverse. I suspect people of plotting to make me happy. ~ J.D. Salinger

Day 335: I have no faith in human perfectibility. I think that human exertion will have no appreciable effect upon humanity. Man is only more active—not more happy—nor more wise than he was 6000 years ago. ~ Edgar Allen Poe

Day 336: If only we'd stop trying to be happy, we could have a pretty good time. ~ Edith Wharton

Day 337: With mirth and laughter let old wrinkles come. ~ William Shakespeare

Day 338: I am choosing happiness over suffering, I know I am. I'm making space for the unknown future to fill up my life with yet-to-come-surprises. ~ Ellizabeth Gilbert, author of Eat, Pray, Love

Day 339: I am the happiest creature in the world. Perhaps other people have said so before, but not one with such justice. I am happier even than Jane; she only smiles, I laugh.~ Jane Austen

Day 340: When the first baby laughed for the first time, its laugh broke into a thousand pieces, and they all went skipping about, and that was the beginning of fairies. ~ J.M. Barrie, author of Peter Pan

Day 341: I, not events, have the power to make me happy or unhappy today. I can choose which it shall be. Yesterday is dead, tomorrow hasn't arrived yet. I have just one day, today, and I'm going to be happy in it. ~ Groucho Marx

Day 342: I don't think there are any limits to how excellent we could make life seem. ~ Jonathan Safran Foer

Day 343: I heard a definition once: Happiness is health and short memory! I wish I'd invented it, because it's true. ~ Audrey Hepburn

Day 344: That;s the difference between me and the rest of the world! Happiness is good enough for me! I demand euphoria! ~ Bill Watterson

Day 345: Actual happiness looks pretty squalid in comparison with the overcompensations for misery. And of course, stability isn't nearly so spectacular as instability. And being contented has none of the glamour of a good fight against misfortune, none of the picturesqueness of a struggle with temptation, or a fatal overthrow by passion or doubt. Happiness is never grand. ~ Aldous Huxley

Day 346: There are two ways to get enough. One is to continue to accumulate more and more. The other is to desire less. ~ G.K. Chesterton

Day 347: What if some day or night a demon were to steal after you into your loneliest loneliness and say to you: "This life as you now live it and have lived it, you will have to live once more and innumerable times more"…Would you not throw yourself down and gnash your teeth and curse the demon who spoke thus? Or have you once experienced a tremendous moment when you have answered him: "You are a god and never have I head of anything more divine." ~ Freidrich Nietzsche

Day 348: A mathematical formula for happiness: Reality divided by expectations. There were two ways to be happy: improve your reality or lower your expectations. ~ Jodi Picoult

Day 349: I think happiness is what makes you pretty. Period. Happy people are beautiful. They become like a mirror and they reflect their happiness. ~ Drew Barrymore

Day 350: Let no one ever come to you without leaving better and happier. Be the living expression of God's kindness: kindness in your face, kindness in your eyes, and kindness in your smile. ~ Mother Teresa

Day 351: The happiness of your life depends on the quality of your thoughts. ~ Marcus Aurelius

Day 352: I know that's what people say—you'll get over it. I'd say it too. But I know it's not true. Oh, you'll be happy again, never fear. But you won't forget. Every time you fall in love it will be because something in the man reminds you of him. ~ Betty Smith

Day 353: The secret of happiness is freedom, the secret of freedom is courage. ~ Carrie Jones

Day 354: Every man has his secret sorrows to which the world knows not; and oftentimes we call a man cold when he is only sad. ~ Henry Wadsworth Longfellow

Day 355: Happiness makes up in height for what it lacks in strength. ~ Robert Frost

Day 356: One of the keys to happiness is a bad memory. ~ Rita Mae Brown

Day 357: Happiness depends upon ourselves. ~ Aristotle

Day 358: Generally speaking, the most miserable people I know are those who are obsessed with themselves; the happiest people I know are those who lose themselves with the service of others…By and large, I have come to see that if we complain about life, it is because we are only thinking of ourselves. ~ Gordon B. Hinckley

Day 359: It's like Tolstoy said. Happiness is an allegory, unhappiness is a story. ~ Haruki Murakami

Day 360: Please believe that things are good with me, and even when they're not, they will be soon enough. And I will always believe the same about you. ~ Stephen Chbosky

Day 361: Now and then it's good to pause in our pursuit of happiness and just be happy. ~ Guillaume Apollinaire

Day 362: The worst part of success is trying to find someone who is happy for you. ~ Bette Midler

Day 363: So we shall let the reader answer this question for himself: who is the happier man, he who has braved the storm of life and lived or he who has stayed securely on shore and merely existed? ~ Hunter S. Thompson

Day 364: Even if the happiness forgets you a little bit, never completely forget about it. ~ Jacques Prevert

Day 365: The Constitution only guarantees the American people the right to pursue happiness. You have to catch it yourself. ~ Author unknown

If you enjoyed reading this book you may also enjoy

The entire collection of 365 Days of Happiness Books

365 Days of America
365 Days of Cats
365 Days of Dogs
365 Days of Happiness
365 Days of Horses
365 Days of Romance
365 Days of Sports
365 Days of Writing
365 Days of the Bible

Made in the USA
Lexington, KY
17 April 2014